THE
360 DEGREE FEEDBACK
POCKETBOOK

By Tony Peacock

Drawings by Phil Hailstone

GW00498919

Published by:
Management Pocketbooks Ltd
Laurel House, Station Approach, Alresford, Hants SO24 9JH, U.K.
Tel: +44 (0)1962 735573   Fax: +44 (0)1962 733637
E-mail: sales@pocketbook.co.uk
Website: www.pocketbook.co.uk

This edition published 2007.

British Library Cataloguing-in-Publication Data – A catalogue record for this book is available
from the British Library.

ISBN 978 1 903776 79 7

Design, typesetting and graphics by **efex ltd**. Printed in U.K.

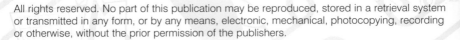

CONTENTS

1NTRODUCTION

INTRODUCTION

360 DEGREE FEEDBACK

Effectively run, 360 degree feedback is a brilliant way to motivate people, achieve business goals, help people build on their strengths, address personal development needs and develop their careers.

This book is for anyone who is interested in introducing such a process into their organisation, or who wants to further develop or invigorate an existing scheme. It will also be of great use to managers who have to facilitate a 360 review feedback session and want to know how to use the system to best effect. Finally, it will benefit anyone who is to be a 360 review subject, as it will give a thorough understanding of what such a review is meant to achieve and how to get the most from it.

In these pages you will find out how to design and introduce a successful scheme; how to get full participation; how to produce effective 360 review reports and conduct successful feedback interviews; how to develop appropriate personal development plans, together with a host of tips and ideas to ensure your 360 degree feedback system is a successful and motivating process.

INTRODUCTION

THE BASIC CONCEPT

A 360 degree feedback review provides people with constructive feedback on how their work-based behaviour is seen by their colleagues. It is primarily for personal development but can be used for other purposes.

Feedback is collected from workmates who are asked to complete a non-attributable questionnaire that explores how the review subject goes about their work. Feedback is usually collected electronically via email or the web. The information received in the questionnaires is combined into a report of charts, graphs, tables and written comments, that are fed back to the review subject, either by their suitably trained manager or by a performance coach, who will help them to develop an action plan based on the feedback.

It is called a **360** review because responses will come from people all around the review subject – their manager, peers and other co-workers, team members, even their clients and customers can all play a constructive part in providing them with valuable feedback on how they are perceived.

LINK TO TRADITIONAL APPRAISAL

360 degree feedback is often used as a **stand alone** personal development process that focuses on developing skills and addressing development needs. It can also be used however, to **enhance** a traditional appraisal or performance review.

Traditional reviews typically cover:

- The performance of the review subject in the **past** – what they have achieved and how they have gone about their work
- **Future** objectives – their organisational and personal goals
- What **support and development** they need to achieve their future objectives

LINK TO TRADITIONAL APPRAISAL

When it comes to 360 feedback, most contacts, with the exception of the manager, won't know how well an individual has performed against their business or personal objectives. 360 feedback therefore tends to focus on providing information on **behavioural** aspects of the review subject: *how* they do things, rather than *what* they do. Such feedback leads to a much better informed appraisal discussion.

Where organisational objectives are agreed and reviewed at a team level, 360 review can even **replace** traditional appraisal.

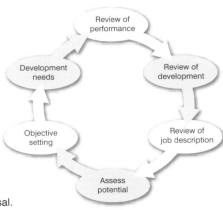

Review of performance

Review of development

Development needs

Review of job description

Objective setting

Assess potential

REVEALING THE 'BLIND SPOT'

An effective level of self-awareness is a starting point for high-level performance in any field. A simple model of self-awareness is the 'JoHari window' (named after the first names of its inventors, Joseph Luft and Harry Ingham). This splits human interaction into four segments:

1. The **open** quadrant represents things that the individual knows about themselves, and that others know about them.

2. The **blind spot** represents things that other people know about a person, which the person is unaware of.

3. The **hidden** quadrant represents things that people know about themselves but that others do not know.

4. The **unknown potential** quadrant represents things that are unknown to the individual and to others.

A 360 review provides a person with valuable feedback from others, thus opening up the 'blind spot' as well as encouraging them to share information from their 'hidden' quadrant. A well facilitated feedback review will also help unlock the 'unknown potential'.

REVEALING THE 'BLIND SPOT'

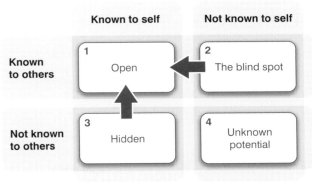

	Known to self	Not known to self
Known to others	1 Open	2 The blind spot
Not known to others	3 Hidden	4 Unknown potential

➡ = effect of 360 review

BENEFITS OF 360 TO THE INDIVIDUAL

- Review subjects receive constructive feedback on areas of their performance that they don't receive by any other means
- Feedback can be obtained from a wide range of people who don't normally contribute to an individual's development
- More open and relevant feedback can be obtained than is gained from traditional appraisal – for example, some skill areas, such as leadership, are often better judged by those being led than by the leader's manager
- The review subject gains self-awareness as they take a 'reality check' on their self-perception – feedback is difficult to ignore when expressed consistently by a number of colleagues
- Relationship with their manager can be improved through greater understanding
- Feedback shows how they are valued and hence improves motivation
- Review subjects have the opportunity to discuss their feedback, often with an independent performance coach who can help them analyse the comments and decide on action points

INTRODUCTION

BENEFITS TO THE MANAGER & THE ORGANISATION

- Managers gain a more rounded picture of the review subject's skills and knowledge
- Communication between managers and review subjects is enhanced
- Reviews act as development needs analysis within teams
- Managers understand what they need to do to support their people
- Giving 360 feedback helps respondents develop their communication skills
- The process can build a culture of mutual respect and responsibility for helping others grow
- Participants learn to focus on the core organisational competencies that affect business performance
- Useful in 'flat' organisations where managers may have a large number of direct reports, none of whom they interact with enough to give them a rounded picture of their performance
- The process provides an input to talent management

USES FOR 360 REVIEW

- To give people more self-awareness
- To develop people in their jobs
- As an input to a personal development programme
- As part of a more general appraisal process
- To identify talent and succession planning

- As part of career progression
- For organisational change processes
- As support for outplacement
- Pre and/or post training needs analysis (TNA)
- For team development

Whatever reason you have for doing it, it is important that you make it absolutely clear to all concerned at the beginning of the process, as this will have an impact on both the design and delivery of your system. You need to be vigilant in maintaining the spirit of the process throughout.

GETTING STARTED

KNOWING WHY

It is important to be clear why you are running a 360 review scheme. Having identified your reasons, you need to be methodical in introducing and running the scheme.

A well planned scheme will allow review subjects to gain considerable benefit and they will come back for more in the future.

Set objectives

Determine competencies

Develop system

Undertake training and briefing

Collect feedback

Produce the report

Give coaching feedback

Create personal development plan

GETTING STARTED

THE PLAYERS

- The scheme facilitator – the person who organises the review
- The review subject – the person having the review
- The review subject's manager
- Respondents – anyone who provides feedback to the review subject
- The feedback coach – the person who will communicate the results of the review to the review subject

APPOINT A TALENTED FACILITATOR

No matter how automated your scheme is, there will still be administration involved: distribution lists to set up; questionnaires to distribute and collect; queries to answer; people to remind; reports to organise and feedback sessions to timetable.

An external 360 supplier will be able to provide some of this support, but at least one dedicated person should be appointed within the organisation to facilitate the process and liaise with everyone involved.

The facilitator will need good organisational skills, together with tact, diplomacy and the ability to motivate everyone to play their part within the timescale. There are two important functions the facilitator should always undertake if an external provider is not being used:

- Ensuring the review subject chooses appropriate respondents
- Supervising the audit trail of who provides what information – important if there are any problems with the process

A good facilitator should make the process appear easy to follow, not a chore.

GO IT ALONE OR FIND EXTERNAL HELP?

The first decision you need to make is whether you want to develop your own 360 review system or to use the services of one of the many external providers who offer their own system.

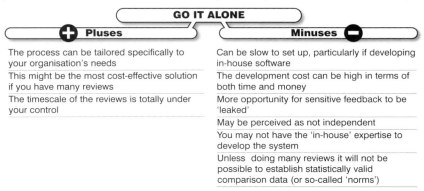

GO IT ALONE

➕ Pluses	➖ Minuses
The process can be tailored specifically to your organisation's needs	Can be slow to set up, particularly if developing in-house software
This might be the most cost-effective solution if you have many reviews	The development cost can be high in terms of both time and money
The timescale of the reviews is totally under your control	More opportunity for sensitive feedback to be 'leaked'
	May be perceived as not independent
	You may not have the 'in-house' expertise to develop the system
	Unless doing many reviews it will not be possible to establish statistically valid comparison data (or so-called 'norms')

FIND EXTERNAL HELP

Depending on the amount of external support you feel you need, you can look for a company that simply provides you with generic 360 review software or one that offers a fully managed process using their own online system, facilitation and coaching.

USE AN EXTERNAL PROVIDER

Pluses	Minuses
Can provide a proven system without any software glitches	May not be capable of being tailored to your organisation's competency model
Will have experience in running reviews	May not have all the features you want
Can be very cost-effective as charges are often on a fixed 'cost per review' basis	Can be expensive if a tailored system is commissioned for you
Independent of the organisation so worries about bias or confidentiality can be minimised	May not be properly validated
Data is collected externally thus reducing the possibility of 'leakage' (or perception of leakage) of the source of feedback	

CHOOSING A PARTNER

If you decide to use an external provider, you need to ask prospective partners:

- How easy is their system to use?
- Can it be customised to use your own competency model?
- Does the system provide security, so that only invited respondents can participate?
- Is there an audit trail so that the scheme facilitator can identify who has, or has not, completed the questionnaire?
- Can they provide briefings, training and help files if required?
- Does their system automatically check that questionnaires are completed properly and that questions have not been left unanswered?
- Do they have appropriate processes in place to safeguard the security of the feedback and to comply with data protection legislation?
- Is there data on the reliability and validity of their questionnaire?
- Can you 'badge' the questionnaire with your logo rather than theirs?
- Is there a personal contact to deal with the inevitable queries?
- Who owns the copyright to the data collected?

WINNING COMMITMENT & OVERCOMING RESISTANCE

The success of your scheme will depend to a large extent on the degree of 'buy in' you are able to get for the process from all concerned. It should **not** be seen as the latest initiative from the HR team. All participants will need to understand the benefits of the scheme, how it works and how they can contribute to its success.

- Win commitment from senior managers. They are likely to be actively involved as both review subjects and respondents and will be able to encourage others
- Stress the link to business performance
- Involve people in identifying the benefits and in designing the process
- Make it part of your organisation's strategic activities
- Ensure enough resources are devoted to it for marketing it properly
- Run training/briefing on the process for everyone who will be involved
- Use your team briefing or weekly team meeting to educate people
- Hold face to face briefing/training sessions for review subjects
- Consult with trade unions if appropriate and gain their support

GETTING STARTED

BRIEFING & TRAINING PARTICIPANTS

Everyone involved in 360 feedback needs to understand why it is being done,
how it works and what they need to do to fully participate. This will involve various
activities including:

- Publicity about the scheme in newsletters, 'in-house' magazines, etc
- Face to face training and briefing where there is the opportunity for people
  to ask questions
- Preparation of guidance notes with the answers to FAQs (frequently asked
  questions) circulated electronically and in hard copy
- Information on the scheme on your intranet site
- A list of relevant external internet links where people can find general information
  about 360 review
- Nominated individuals in your organisation who can provide information

THE BRIEFING/TRAINING PROGRAMME

Cover the following in your briefing/training:

- What 360 review is
- Why you are doing it and what will be the benefits to the review subject and the wider organisation
- How the scheme will operate in your organisation
- How it will fit in with more general appraisal processes
- Who will be involved
- How people should participate
- How anonymity will be maintained
- How feedback will be provided
- What the feedback report will look like
- Who will see the feedback report
- What the expected outcomes are
- Where to get further information

INVOLVING THE REVIEW SUBJECT

In the best 360 reviews the review subject feels an ownership of the process rather than that something is being 'done to them' by the HR or training department. You can encourage ownership in the following ways:

- Involve review subjects in early exploration of how it will benefit them
- Consider making the process voluntary at first. The 'early adopters' will soon convince others of its benefits
- Get review subjects to nominate the people who will provide them with feedback
- Involve them in sending out the invitations to participate
- Encourage them to help with the administration of the scheme and chase up respondents
- Ensure that they take the lead, assisted by the feedback coach, in developing a personal development plan arising from the feedback

INVOLVING THE REVIEW SUBJECT

Some schemes take the involvement even further by allowing the review subject to run their own review, using automated software where they enter their contact details into the system, trigger invitations to take part along with personalised messages, monitor who has responded and send reminders.

What the review subject **won't** be able to do in such schemes is to see the responses that come back from the individual respondents. These will only be available to the scheme administrator who compiles the final feedback report.

This 'self-administered' scheme should only be done, however, where the review subject has a high level of personal commitment to the process and is willing to take on the administrative burden.

KEY CONCERNS – ANONYMITY

People are often more willing to offer honest feedback if they know their contributions will be non-attributable, ie the review subject will not know who has said what. The review subject will know who was invited to take part, but they will not be able to identify individual comments.

You can ensure that feedback is non-attributable by:

- Ensuring your feedback gathering process is 'leak proof'. This is easy if you are using an external agency; with an internal process make sure your scheme facilitator is the only person to process the feedback questionnaires

- Mentioning in your pre-briefing to respondents that they may wish to phrase their feedback in a way that doesn't identify them personally

- Ensuring there are several respondents in each respondent category you set up

- Separating out different points from any specific respondent in the feedback report, so that they are less likely to be identified from blocks of comments

- Encouraging review subjects to concentrate on the **content** of the feedback, not on guessing who said it

(27)

FEEDBACK FROM THE REVIEW SUBJECT'S MANAGER

There is one important exception when it comes to anonymity that relates to the **ratings feedback** received from the review subject's own manager. Often there will only be one person in the category of 'manager' in a review. While any later written comments offered by that manager will typically be combined with those of others, the **rating scores** they give will usually be separately identifiable in the charts in the report.

This is right and proper. Part of the role of a good manager is to provide **direct feedback** to their team members and to discuss with them how they perceive their performance. If a manager is not prepared to have his or her scores identified in the review then the review probably shouldn't be taking place.

TIMING OF REVIEWS

Reviews can be held:

- Before a traditional appraisal review to inform the discussion on strengths and development needs
- After a traditional appraisal to help formulate a personal development plan to help achieve business goals
- As part of a personal development programme
- Before a training programme to provide feedback on key areas to focus on
- As an input to an assessment centre
- Before, or shortly after, promotion to help identify the skills needed to develop into a new role
- When establishing a new project team or building an existing one
- During an outplacement programme

FREQUENCY OF REVIEWS

There is a considerable amount of work involved in setting up and running a 360 review. Lots of people will be involved in giving feedback and the resulting personal development plan or other action plan is likely to take months to carry out. Reviews should typically be undertaken on not less than an **annual** basis.

There may be occasions when a shorter time span is appropriate, such as with a change of role in an organisation, but care should be taken not to invoke 360 review 'fatigue' on the part of respondents who are repeatedly asked to provide feedback to the same people.

SHARING THE FEEDBACK REPORT

You need to have a clear understanding at the **beginning** of the review process as to who will see the feedback report and what will happen to it. People who should automatically see it are:

- The **scheme facilitator**, who will collate the feedback. This person will most likely have a reviewing role to ensure questionnaires have been completed properly and are correctly processed into the final report
- The **feedback coach**, who will work with the review subject in analysing the report, to spot key themes
- The **review subject** (unbelievably there are some organisations that don't allow the review subject to see the feedback report!)

SHARING THE FEEDBACK REPORT

Others who **might** see the feedback report, with prior agreement, are:

- Someone in the organisation who might be co-ordinating an overall report on the 360 review scheme or its outcomes
- Trainers who are using the 360 review as an input to a programme
- Review panellists, if the process is part of a development programme or an assessment process
- Team members, if the review is part of a team review and this has been previously agreed

In all cases it needs to be clear to everyone **before** the process starts who will see the information.

SHARING FEEDBACK WITH THE MANAGER

The 360 review is primarily a **personal** development process and so it is not necessarily appropriate that the review subject's manager sees the full feedback report. What is more common is that the manager will be involved in the discussion of the personal development plan arising from the review, perhaps supported by a summary of the report to understand the thinking behind the action points.

There are, however, situations where the manager **will** see all of the feedback report:

● If they are to act as the feedback coach

● Where they are involved in a follow-up coaching role with the review subject

● Where the 360 process forms part of a wider appraisal or other development activity

In all these situations the manager should be properly briefed/trained to understand how to interpret the feedback and provide coaching support to the review subject.

TEST THE PROCESS

To ensure people have confidence in the process you should always begin by testing it with volunteers. A pilot scheme with four or five people will:

- Help iron out any technical bugs or administrative difficulties

- Find out if the questionnaire is user friendly

- Allow you to see if your report, with its graphs, charts and tables, is easily understood by your review subjects

- Judge how useful the process is to the review subject

- Help promote the process amongst participants

DESIGNING THE PROCESS

WHO TO INVOLVE IN PROVIDING FEEDBACK

It is called 360 feedback because the feedback is provided by people all around the review subject. These people might include:

- The review subject's manager
- Other more senior managers they interact with
- Partners/executive/board members
- Peers – colleagues at a similar level in the organisation
- Team members/direct reports
- Other key work contacts
- Clients and customers
- Other external contacts

IDENTIFYING CATEGORIES OF RESPONDENT

The questionnaire will ask the respondent to select a relationship category that best describes their working relationship to the review subject. This allows for the feedback report to reflect possible differences of perspective.

Typical groupings are:

- The review subject
- The review subject's manager(s) and other more senior managers
- Peers
- Direct reports
- Other respondents

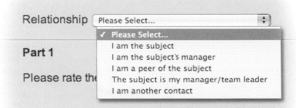

Relationship | Please Select... |

✓ Please Select...
I am the subject
I am the subject's manager
I am a peer of the subject
The subject is my manager/team leader
I am another contact

Part 1

Please rate th

DESIGNING THE PROCESS

CHOOSING RESPONDENTS

In development reviews the most obvious person to identify respondents is the review subject. They will have a perception of who their most important key contacts are, and by being empowered to make their own choices, they are more likely to be open to the feedback given.

It may be appropriate for the review subject's manager to approve the invite list but the subject is much less likely to accept feedback from people they feel have been 'imposed' on them.

Some respondents would automatically be included, for example their manager and some of their direct reports. After that they should aim to nominate people who can provide them with as rounded a picture as possible. In particular they should be encouraged to choose those who may give them fresh insights. There is little point in them only selecting their work friends as they are likely to offer a limited perspective.

The scheme facilitator should ensure that the appropriate number and range of respondents are selected in a timely manner.

DESIGNING THE QUESTIONNAIRE

Generally, most respondents are not in a position to offer feedback on what a review subject **achieves** (with the notable exception of the subject's manager!). 360 feedback typically focuses on how people **behave** on a day to day basis; the work **activities** they undertake, and suggestions on what **changes** they should make in the future. Questionnaires typically ask respondents to do the following:

- Rate the review subject's skills, knowledge and attitude against agreed competencies:
  'How often does he/she coach and mentor others?'
  hardly ever ○ occasionally ○ sometimes ○ frequently ○ almost always

- Provide opinions on the importance of a particular competency for the review subject in their role:
  'How important an activity is this for him/her?'
  not important ○ slightly important ○ important ○ very important ○ essential ○

- Offer suggestions on the review subject and their role:
  'What should they do more of?' 'What are their key strengths?'

(39)

CHOOSING COMPETENCIES TO ASK ABOUT

Competency definition: an observable cluster of skills, knowledge and attitude required to achieve a desired objective.

Your organisation may well have its own competency model, in which case it is easy to incorporate this into a 360 review questionnaire. For those without their own framework, there are generic competency models that can be used. While these are unlikely to be as focused on your organisation's key performance areas as a framework developed specifically for you, they can be useful in prompting general reflection on the review subject's performance, as well as acting as a prompt when answering 'open' questions. Typically generic models will cover areas such as:

- Teamworking
- Interpersonal skills
- Communication
- Representation
- Planning and reviewing
- Development and strategy

- Job knowledge
- Motivation
- Resilience
- Customer/client focus
- Quality orientation

EXPLORING COMPETENCIES

A person's level of performance in any competency is explored by asking respondents to rate them against competency **items**. The average of the rating scores achieved for these items gives an indication of the overall performance level for that competency.

TEAMWORKING ITEMS

Encourages a team approach

Effectively leads own team

Gives praise to the team for work well done

Shows concern for team spirit

Is a team player

VALIDITY OF QUESTIONS

The questions you ask need to be appropriate to the review subject. In choosing questions you should ask yourself:

- Does what's being measured predict anything about the review subject's job performance?

- Are the questions relevant to the review subject's job?

- Is there a good 'face validity', ie does the question look like it measures the competency being explored?

- Do results from different review subjects differentiate between levels of performance?

- Are the tests and retests consistent over time?

External consultants are often able to use comparison information from other organisations to help ensure validity.

CHOOSE YOUR LANGUAGE

Avoid:

✗ Statements that cover more than one point –
'Is a good team player and works hard at maintaining team spirit'

✗ Long-winded statements –
'Works hard at trying to convey key communication messages from senior management to their team and other key contacts both within and external to the team and organisation'

✗ Items that are open to interpretation –
'Uses appropriate interventions to handle conflict' (what does appropriate mean here?)

✗ Double negatives –
'Does not dismiss others' ideas'

✗ Technical or complex vocabulary that may not be familiar to respondents –
'Facilitates proactive discourse between corporate stakeholders'

Where respondents may not have English as a first language, consider accurately translating the questionnaire.

DISTRIBUTING STATEMENTS IN THE QUESTIONNAIRE

If you list all of the statements about a particular competence in one single block in your questionnaire there is a good chance that there will be a 'halo' or 'horns' effect, with similar scores being given to each item. It is better to space out individual items relating to a particular competence throughout this section of the questionnaire.

1. Encourages a team approach
2. Is open and fair in dealings with others
3. Speaks persuasively in meetings and presentations
4. Is well organised in own approach to work
5. Contributes well to the development of the organisation's business plans

DESIGNING THE PROCESS

CHOOSING A RATING SCALE

The most common way of scoring competence is on a 'rating scale', where people tick a particular point on a scale to indicate their level of agreement with a statement.
A scale of at least five options offers the ability to differentiate performance levels in a way that assists discussion at the feedback stage. Typical scales are:

Agreement scale
strongly disagree ◯   disagree ◯   undecided ◯   agree ◯   strongly agree ◯

Frequency scale
hardly ever ◯   occasionally ◯   sometimes ◯   frequently ◯   almost always ◯

Effectiveness scale
not effective ◯   less effective ◯   effective ◯   very effective ◯   extremely effective ◯

Importance scale
not important ◯   slightly important ◯   important ◯   very important ◯   essential ◯

Quality scale
needs significant improvement ◯   needs improvement ◯   typical ◯   good ◯
excels/role model ◯

AVOID NUMERICAL SCALES

Some systems use a numerical scale
for people to rate performance such as:

Numerical scores can, however,
be difficult to interpret at the
feedback stage (what does a
score of 6 actually mean?)
and can lead to an over-reliance
on the numbers as a focus
for discussion.

BALANCED SCALES

Try to ensure your scale offers a realistic range of options.

- Avoid scales that are positively balanced:
  excellent/ very good/ good/ average/ poor
- Avoid scales that are negatively balanced:
  good/ average/ poor/ very poor/ awful
- Don't use scales that use absolutes such
  as *never* or *always* as their end points;
  these don't get used

DESIGNING THE PROCESS

DON'T KNOW!

However close the working relationship is with colleagues, there may be areas of performance where the respondent doesn't feel they know the review subject well enough to be able to offer a meaningful response to a particular question.

There should always be a choice of *'cannot say'*, *'don't know'*, *'no experience'* or *'unknown'* for respondents who may not have seen the review subject using a particular set of skills.

<table>
<tr><td>SCORE</td></tr>
<tr><td>1 Hardly ever</td></tr>
<tr><td>2 Occasionally</td></tr>
<tr><td>3 Sometimes</td></tr>
<tr><td>4 Frequently</td></tr>
<tr><td>5 Almost always</td></tr>
<tr><td>U Unknown</td></tr>
</table>

	1	2	3	4	5	U
21. Gives praise to the team for work well done	○	○	○	○	○	○
22. Is timely and effective in dealing with conflict and grievances	○	○	○	○	○	○
23. Is a good negotiator	○	○	○	○	○	○
24. Effectively coordinates the efforts of own team towards objectives	○	○	○	○	○	○
25. Effectively uses management account information	○	○	○	○	○	○

DESIGNING THE PROCESS

IMPORTANCE TO THE INDIVIDUAL'S ROLE

Unless you are designing a questionnaire specifically tailored to a review subject, it is possible that a particular questionnaire item may not be very significant for that individual. You might therefore want to ask for views on this by including an 'importance' scale. Responses to such questions can help the review subject to concentrate their development on the areas that are seen as most important.

Example:

'Develops new services to meet customer/client needs'

Not important ○   slightly important ○   important ○
very important ○   essential ○

Some questionnaires omit this type of question on the basis that it adds to the overall length of the process and that discussion on the importance of items will come out in the feedback session.

OPEN QUESTIONS

Well designed 'open' questions give respondents the opportunity to offer **qualitative** feedback that can provide excellent insights into feedback elsewhere in the questionnaire. Asking the right questions is critical to getting meaningful feedback that will help the review subject to understand what others are saying in their ratings.

- Use **open** questions: what; why; when; how; where; who
- Ask **constructive** questions: *'What are the review subject's key development needs?'* not: *'What is the review subject bad at?'*
- Give respondents the opportunity to add other feedback: *'Please add any other constructive comments you feel it would be useful for the review subject to have.'*

Examples of constructive questions

What are the review subject's key strengths?
What are their key development issues?
What other constructive feedback can you offer?

What should the review subject do more of?
What should they continue doing?
What should they do less of?

What should the review subject start doing?
What should they stop doing?

PROVIDING GUIDANCE

Providing written feedback to others may well be a new experience for many of those involved, and so it can be useful to provide some guidance and written examples. This could be an accompanying document, provided as a web link or included in the questionnaire.

The guidance should stress that the more people write, the more effective their feedback is. Ask people to try to identify a minimum of **three** points for each question.

What are Errol's key strengths?

Errol has a clear vision of where the organisation is going – future developments, ideas, etc. He communicates this well through all of the briefings he provides for us.

He has incredible enthusiasm and drive for change and is always willing to take time to motivate others towards developing our services.

Errol always makes time for members of staff when they have queries or need assistance and is always fair in his decisions. He goes out of his way to ensure people have understood the guidance he has provided.

51

AUTOMATING THE PROCESS

Although it is possible for you to circulate a paper questionnaire, many organisations now circulate them via the internet or email. The advantages are:

- It's easier to distribute and collect questionnaires
- Respondents can easily complete the questionnaire online in their own time
- The processing of the questionnaires into the final report can be done easily and speedily
- The confidentiality of responses is improved
- Automated processes have a much higher response rate than paper based systems

Options:

- Get your IT development team to help set up a system
- Buy 360 feedback software with a built-in internet facility and customise it to your own competencies
- Use an external 360 feedback consultant to set up the system for you
- Use an established questionnaire, again available from external consultants

MAKE IT EASY TO COMPLETE

Respondents in 360 reviews are busy people. You therefore want to design the questionnaire so that you can extract the maximum amount of feedback from them in the minimum amount of time. This is particularly true when several reviews are taking place in an organisation at the same time and people may be asked to complete more than one questionnaire.

- Have short, clear instructions
- Show an example of how to complete one of the competency item questions
- Try to have all the questions on one electronic page so that people can see everything they have to complete
- If you can't have all the questions on one page have a progress bar that shows how much has been completed
- Let people know where to get more information about the process

NUMBER OF QUESTIONS

A good 360 review will offer the review subject feedback across all the key areas of their work performance. There needs, however, to be a balance between the number of questions asked and the amount of time it takes to complete the questionnaire. It is reckoned that about 80% of 360 review questionnaires contain 50 or fewer questions.

Shorter questionnaires tend to get a much higher response rate. You should aim to have a questionnaire that can be fully completed in 10 – 15 minutes.

DESIGNING THE PROCESS

SECURITY ON THE INTERNET

Ensure that a questionnaire is only completed by those you want to involve by:

- Sending the questionnaire directly to each respondent
- Forwarding them a personal link to the online questionnaire
- Sending them a password to access the questionnaire
- Having an audit trail so the scheme facilitator can trace the origin of any response; this is also useful if anything goes wrong with the process or there is the need to follow up
- Using a system that automatically logs when people send in their completed questionnaires; this also helps with identifying who needs to be reminded

DESIGN YOUR OWN QUESTIONNAIRE

If you decide to use an external partner to help you design the review, or if you buy specialised 360 feedback software, you are likely to be able to use a battery of pre-designed competency items to help you customise your questionnaire. This is particularly useful if you do not have your own competency model or you wish to customise a questionnaire to a particular individual or group for whom you don't have your own appropriate competency items.

Competencies used may be agreed centrally in conjunction with the HR or personnel teams. Some systems allow the **review subject** to design their own questionnaire by selecting from the battery of pre-designed competency questions. This allows a high level of customisation but relies on the review subject having a good understanding of the key competencies that affect their performance.

DESIGN YOUR OWN QUESTIONNAIRE

EXAMPLE

Choosing your competencies

As well as the core organisational competencies, you must choose between 3 and 6 optional competencies that you want to receive feedback on.

Tick those that you want included in your review.

Leadership
The ability to harness the skills and knowledge of others in a co-ordinated way so as to produce an effective team focused on organisational objectives

Core competency

Team working
The ability to work effectively as part of a team

Core competency

Verbal communication
The ability to communicate knowledge and ideas in a clear and concise manner

Core competency

DESIGNING THE PROCESS

DESIGN YOUR OWN QUESTIONNAIRE
EXAMPLE

Optional competencies

Personal motivation
The ability to maintain enthusiasm and communicate that enthusiasm to others even in times of adversity

Creativity
The ability to generate new ideas and apply solutions in novel ways and new situations

Self-development
The ability to seek to learn from experiences and develop your skills and knowledge

Business focus
The ability to seek out and pursue business opportunities that accord with corporate goals

MAKING IT WORK

SELF-COMPLETION OF QUESTIONNAIRE

Review subjects will normally be invited to complete the questionnaire about themselves.

The benefits are:

- Critically analysing their own strengths and development needs will help them focus on what they need to do in the future to develop their skills and knowledge

- The process will help them think about how other respondents have completed the questionnaire

- It will allow them to contrast their self-image with the image the other respondents have of them

- Their answers will provide topics to discuss with their feedback coach

EXTERNAL RESPONDENTS

External clients, customers and other contacts can be invited to participate but there are some important considerations:

- They may be reluctant to offer feedback if they feel they don't know the review subject very well
- They may be cautious about offering feedback that they feel would jeopardise their working relationship with the review subject
- They may not be able to offer meaningful feedback on some areas of performance
- They can be more difficult to brief on the process

Ideas to help with this:

- Only invite external respondents where there has been a close working relationship, say as part of a project team
- Stress the confidential, non-attributable nature of the feedback
- Make it clear that they can use the 'don't know' option for some answers
- Have a more limited questionnaire for circulation to external contacts only

NUMBER OF RESPONDENTS

The objective is to gather feedback from sufficient people to offer a rounded picture of how the review subject is perceived. A group of 9 to 12 respondents is typical:

- Fewer than this and it is difficult to get sufficient breadth of views to offer comprehensive feedback

- It is difficult for the review subject to deny that the feedback is representative when coming from this many people

- In this size of group key points will typically be repeated, thus adding emphasis to key strengths and development areas

- Having several people in each reporting category helps to keep scores non-attributable

- Having more than 12 people adds to the administrative burden of running the review and doesn't usually offer much in the way of additional insights

MAKING IT WORK

THE INVITATION TO TAKE PART

The content of your invitation to participate will influence the response received.

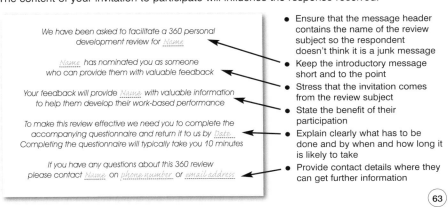

We have been asked to facilitate a 360 personal development review for <u>Name</u>

- Ensure that the message header contains the name of the review subject so the respondent doesn't think it is a junk message

<u>Name</u> has nominated you as someone who can provide them with valuable feedback

- Keep the introductory message short and to the point
- Stress that the invitation comes from the review subject

Your feedback will provide <u>Name</u> with valuable information to help them develop their work-based performance

- State the benefit of their participation

To make this review effective we need you to complete the accompanying questionnaire and return it to us by <u>Date.</u> Completing the questionnaire will typically take you 10 minutes

- Explain clearly what has to be done and by when and how long it is likely to take

If you have any questions about this 360 review please contact <u>Name</u> on <u>phone number</u> or <u>email address</u>

- Provide contact details where they can get further information

INVOLVING THE REVIEW SUBJECT IN THE INVITATION

A good way to ensure a high level of response is to get the **review subject** personally to contact each of their chosen respondents in advance of the questionnaire being circulated, to encourage them to participate.

Dear Yasser,

I'm shortly to undertake a 360 degree personal development review. In this review 12 of the people who have worked closely with me will be asked to complete a questionnaire about me. The results will be compiled into a non-attributable report (I won't know who offered which pieces of feedback), and I will have the opportunity to discuss the report with a performance coach.

As someone I have worked closely with I would appreciate your feedback and I have asked the review facilitator to invite you to be one of my respondents.

You will shortly receive the invitation from ACME development consultants.

Thanks in advance.

ENCOURAGING PARTICIPATION

- Encourage the review subject to nominate respondents they believe will participate
- Stress in the invitation the benefit to the review subject the feedback will provide
- Market the process thoroughly amongst all participants
- Make the questionnaire as simple and quick to complete as possible
- Get the review subject to contact their chosen respondents to encourage them to participate
- Have a contingency in your cut-off date to allow for late returns
- Where respondents are involved in multiple reviews try to timetable them to avoid overlap
- Limit the number of questions. There is a direct correlation between the length of questionnaires and the percentage of people who respond
- Have a well tested and reliable survey system so that respondents don't have to complete the questionnaire more than once because of technical problems

GIVE PEOPLE TIME

Your respondents are likely to be busy people and your request won't necessarily be top of their 'to do' list. You need to give them sufficient time to complete the questionnaire. Two weeks is good; less than this and they may not find time to do it; more than this and it is likely to go to the bottom of their priorities and be forgotten.

Always allow at least a week for late returns.

POSITIVE & NEGATIVE RESPONSES

There are four types of open question responses that can be provided:

Unconditionally positive
'Zak is a great person to work with!'
These types of comments are good morale builders and always appreciated, but don't help Zak to understand what it is he is doing that makes him 'great' so, while important, they have a limited function.

Conditionally positive
'Yasmin always manages to deliver her work projects on time and to budget.'
This type of comment is highly useful as it provides feedback about a specific work responsibility and helps the review subject understand what specific behaviour is valued.

Conditionally negative
'He could do with improving his time management skills. He often seems disorganised and flustered.'
Again useful, as it provides a specific topic for discussion with the feedback coach.

Unconditionally negative
'She is a complete waste of space!'
Very unhelpful and damaging to the review subject and should be firmly discouraged.

Encourage positive and conditionally negative feedback by offering examples in your guidance notes.

THE IMPACT OF NON-RESPONDENTS

If people don't respond to the invitation to participate, this can have negative effects:

- There is not the **breadth** of feedback that comes with a full level of response
- Key feedback messages may not be reinforced through **repetition** by different respondents
- People who do participate may become **identifiable** if they are the only person in a particular category who takes part

Review subjects may be understandably aggrieved that the colleagues they nominated cannot be bothered to provide them with feedback.

ENCOURAGING QUALITY RESPONSES

Encourage people to provide quality responses by briefing them to:

- Find a time when they can complete the questionnaire without interruption
- Remember they are helping to coach the review subject
- **Reflect** back over a period of months rather than basing feedback on the immediate past
- Provide a minimum of **three** points in response to each open question
- Put points about different behaviours on separate lines
- Provide **evidence** to back up their points
- Focus on **how** the review subject does their job not their general personality
- Reflect on what they value about their colleague and anything they feel it would be useful for them to know
- Keep their comments constructive
- Read through their answers before submission to make sure they will make sense to someone else reading them

REMINDING PEOPLE

Busy people sometimes put aside questionnaires and forget to complete them.

- Ensure your system allows the scheme facilitator to monitor who has replied
- Have a reminder process that gently encourages people to complete the questionnaire
- Have a process for letting review subjects know who hasn't responded and encourage them to contact those people
- In schemes that allow for the review subject to do their own chasing, have a system to remind them

Name	Status
Ali Akbar	Invited
Bernice Bumble	Invited
Charlie Chissom	Invited
Eddie Eagle	Reminded
François Frisson	Reminded
Hari Hodgeson	Completed
Ismail Issaks	Completed
Jermimah Johnson	Completed

OVERCOMING OBJECTIONS

Respondents sometimes decline the invitation to participate. Try to encourage them to take part. Common issues are:

- **Don't have the time** – make the process straightforward and indicate how long it will take; stress the importance of the feedback to the review subject and remind the respondent that they were specifically nominated by the review subject; allow people at least a couple of weeks to respond

- **Don't know the review subject well enough** – stress that although they may only be able to contribute on a limited basis this will be highly useful feedback; remind respondents that there is an option to tick a 'not known' response

- **Don't want to give negative feedback to a colleague** – encourage constructive feedback and reinforce the point that such feedback has been requested by the review subject to help them improve their performance

- **Afraid their comments will be attributable** – reassure them of your security measures to ensure confidentiality

RUNNING MULTIPLE REVIEWS

A single review could typically involve up to 12 respondents, often from within the organisation. 10 simultaneous reviews could therefore involve 120 people or, more likely, the same respondents being asked to complete multiple reviews. It's one thing to have to spend 10 minutes completing a questionnaire, it's quite another to have to do 6 or 8 taking an hour or two!

When you are running multiple reviews, forewarn respondents that they may be asked to complete several questionnaires and consider spreading the start date for reviews that involve the same pool of respondents.

THE FEEDBACK REPORT

THE FEEDBACK REPORT

INTRODUCTION TO THE RESPONDENTS

The feedback report is the most important document in the whole process.
It will be the basis for the feedback discussion and it will form a permanent record
for the review subject.

There are typically three main sections in a 360 review report:

- An introduction that explains the contents of the report

- An analysis of the ratings given – usually presented as graphs or tables of scores

- A record of the written feedback offered

There may also be notes to help the review subject analyse the information and plan
appropriate follow up actions. The report should be written in a clear, understandable
style that communicates immediately without the need for expert interpretation.

THE FEEDBACK REPORT

INTRODUCTION

The feedback report should contain an
introduction that clearly and simply
explains the layout and contents
of the report.

Include:

- The name of the review subject
- The date of the report
- A note about the confidentiality
  of the document
- An outline of each section of the report

COMPARISON OF SCORES FROM RESPONDENT GROUPS

Care should be taken to ensure that the report provides comprehensive information in an easily accessible format. There is no end to the amount of numerical analysis that can be presented in a 360 review feedback report. A successful report presents **key** information and doesn't blind people with statistics.

Your report should show the overall levels of score given by each respondent group for each of the competencies explored. Different colours or patterns can be used to distinguish the different categories of respondent. This will give both the overall level of performance for each one plus easy to view comparisons of relative strengths.

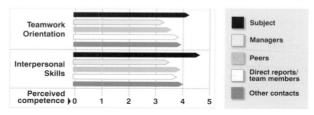

THE FEEDBACK REPORT

REMINDER OF QUESTIONNAIRE ITEMS

To help the review subject understand the competency ratings it is useful to include the statements that were rated in the questionnaire.

Teamwork Orientation

Encourages a team approach
Effectively leads own team
Gives praise to the team for work well done
Shows concern for team spirit
Is a team player

Interpersonal Skills

Is open and fair in dealings with others
Demonstrates effective listening skills
Is timely and effective in dealing with conflict and grievances
Offers recognition and praise to individuals for good work
Mentors and coaches others

THE FEEDBACK REPORT

BREAKDOWN OF SCORES ON COMPETENCY ITEMS

Some 360 review reports stop at the previous level of analysis as it is often enough to prompt a useful discussion at the feedback review. It is possible however to offer further analysis.

At the next level of analysis you can show how the overall score for the competency is made up from the average scores of the individual items for that competency.

This is useful in helping the review subject to understand the overall rating and to see any variations in the scores of the individual items.

	Average
Teamwork Orientation – Overall	4.0
Encourages a team approach	3.8
Effectively leads own team	4.2
Gives praise to the team for work well done	3.6
Shows concern for team spirit	4.4
Is a team player	4.0

SCALE

1. Hardly ever
2. Occasionally
3. Sometimes
4. Frequently
5. Almost always
U. Unknown

THE FEEDBACK REPORT

RANGE OF ANSWERS

A further refinement is to add the range of scores given that make up the average.

	Average	Range
Teamwork Orientation – Overall	4.0	
Encourages a team approach	3.8	3-4
Effectively leads own team	4.2	3-5
Gives praise to the team for work well done	3.6	3-4

Alternatively scores can also be shown visually.

	1	2	3	4	5
Encourages a team approach			◇ ○ △ △	◇ □ △	□ □
Effectively leads own team		◇ △	△ △ △ ◇	○ □	□ □
Gives praise to the team for work well done		△ △	◇ ◇ △ □	○ □	□

○ Self score
◇ Managers
□ Peers
△ Team members

Knowing the spread of scores allows the review subject to appreciate the variation in the responses.

79

THE FEEDBACK REPORT

VARIATIONS IN SCORE ACROSS ITEMS

At the most fundamental level of analysis it is possible
to present the individual scores.

SCALE

1 Hardly ever
2 Occasionally
3 Sometimes
4 Frequently
5 Almost always
U Unknown

	Self	Managers			Peers			Team members			Average excl. self
Mentors and coaches others	2	4	3	2	4	4	U	4	3	5	3.6

This has the advantage of showing variations across different reporting groups as well as
the range of responses given, but can lead to 'analysis paralysis' if too much attention is
paid to individual responses. This is particularly true where there are 50 or 60 individual
competency items being analysed!

Note: While it is normal to show the review subject's own score this is not usually used
in the calculation of the average.

THE FEEDBACK REPORT

AVERAGE AND 'NORM' SCORES

It can be useful to compare the score of an individual with others. Where a group of people in the same organisation and with similar roles are undertaking a 360 review it is possible to calculate the **average** score for the group and present this alongside results achieved by the individual. This allows them to compare themselves with their colleagues. For example, where all the sales staff are being reviewed it is possible to calculate the mean average score across the whole team.

Where there is a directly comparable group from across the industry there may well be a '**norm**' score. This is an industry average, usually derived from hundreds of scores.

	Self	Managers			Peers			Team members			Average excl. self	Team average	Norm group
Mentors and coaches others	2	4	3	2	4	4	U	4	3	5	3.6	3.3	3.2

THE FEEDBACK REPORT

BAR CHARTS & HISTOGRAMS

Data can be provided in lots of ways. For example, bar charts and histograms (column charts) are very good for showing comparisons across competencies and respondent groups.

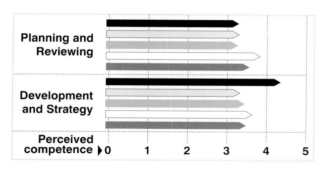

Legend:
- **Subject**
- Managers
- Peers
- Direct reports/team members
- Other contacts

BAR CHARTS & HISTOGRAMS

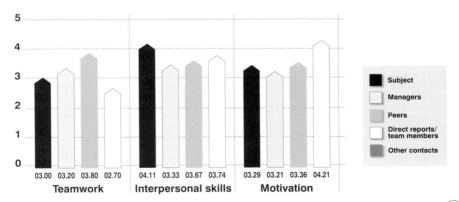

THE FEEDBACK REPORT

RADAR DIAGRAMS

Radar diagrams give an overall summary across all competencies from different reporting groups. Care needs to be taken however as the lines between each point suggests there is a linkage between items where there is not.

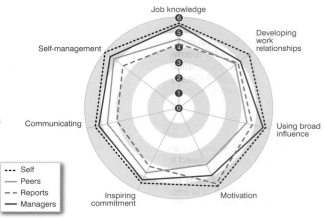

THE FEEDBACK REPORT

LIES, DAMN LIES & STATISTICS!

Graphical representation of feedback scores can be useful in provoking discussion about relative strengths, but take care when interpreting the numerical data. Graphs, charts and tables can assume an importance way beyond any statistical validity they deserve. With an average score for teamworking of 3.9, is the review subject more competent in this area than in communication: score 3.4, when the industry averages are widely different for these two areas? Clearly there is a danger of comparing apples with pears. Even within a single competency area we are often comparing different types of 'apple' with each competency statement.

The same is true of using average scores or 'norms'. Is a 'communication' score of 4.1 for someone in admin comparable with the same score for someone in sales, given the different roles? There are also different types of averages – mean, mode and median. If using averages, you need to check you are comparing like with like.

An average score is only part of the story. Without knowing the spread of scores, or standard deviation, it is impossible to know how different a particular review subject's score is statistically from the average. **Be careful with the numbers!**

THE FEEDBACK REPORT

RANKING OF SCORES

An additional way of highlighting key results is to list the top 10 highest scoring competency items and the bottom 10 scoring items. This will help the review subject to understand the relative strengths of their competencies. If the number of items is not too long the whole ranked list can be provided.

Top 10 scoring items

Demonstrates appropriate emotional control

Writes fluent and understandable emails, memos and reports

Demonstrates a professional image within the organisation and externally

Effectively uses computer systems and software

Demonstrates a high level of knowledge in own work responsibilities

Shows commitment to own job

Stays up to date with developments in own areas of expertise

Bottom 10 scoring items

Shows concern for team spirit

Is a team player

Networks outside the organisation to gather new ideas

Regularly reviews performance of areas under own control

Bases development plans on well-researched information

Seeks to engender a sense of enjoyment and fun in the workplace

Strives to make the organisation an enjoyable place to work

THE FEEDBACK REPORT

WRITTEN FEEDBACK

Responses to open questions often provide the richest source of feedback.

To ensure each point is carefully considered:

- Put each question, with all its answers, on a new page, so the reader concentrates on one question at a time

- If a paragraph of feedback contains several different points separate them out

- Don't print all the respondents' answers in the same order each time, as this might identify them. Eg, don't always put the manager's comments first

- Correct grammar and spelling to make the report look professional, but be careful not to alter the meaning

- Don't change the vocabulary used; these are the words of the respondents and should be read as such

WRITTEN FEEDBACK
EXAMPLE

What are Amy's key strengths?

Amy's technical ability is excellent

Amy's ability to understand the clients' needs, programmes and financial requirements of the project

Her knowledge and expertise in her own field

Amy's good technical knowledge – she's always the person people go to for advice on tricky engineering problems

Amy is patient and calm under pressure

Her technical ability is very high. She always comes up with precise solutions

She responds well to difficult situations and does not shy away from helping to solve problems within the team

Amy is a good communicator; she speaks well in meetings and delivers excellent presentations

Her management of personnel is excellent

She has a nice personality; she never loses her cool

THE FEEDBACK PROCESS

THE FEEDBACK INTERVIEW

There should **always** be the opportunity for the review subject to discuss the feedback **face to face** with someone who has appropriate coaching skills. This could be their manager, if properly experienced in facilitating feedback, or it could be someone else in your organisation, such as a member of your personnel or training team. Alternatively, you could find an external feedback coach to work with them.

Presenting the feedback is often the most critical part of the whole process. If the review is to have a positive impact it is essential that the review subject is able to take on board the information in the constructive way it is intended. Poorly presented feedback can result in the review subject becoming disillusioned and frustrated. They are then unlikely to commit to the process.

THE ROLE OF THE FEEDBACK COACH

- To provide a supportive environment to encourage the review subject to reflect on the feedback provided

- To get the review subject to acknowledge the validity of the views in the feedback as the honest opinions of those expressing them

- To assist the review subject with identifying the behaviours that have given rise to the feedback

- To help the review subject to analyse the feedback and draw out the key themes emerging

- To explore the review subject's response to the feedback

- To assist the review subject to develop an action plan for behavioural change, where this is identified as desirable

THE MANAGER AS FEEDBACK COACH

It is almost always useful for the review subject's manager to be involved in the feedback process, either as a follow up to the formal feedback or, when suitably trained, in the role of feedback coach. This has the following benefits:

- Can lead to greater understanding between the manager and the review subject

- Can develop the manager's coaching skills

- The evidence in the report may make it easier to address areas of common concern

- An action plan is more likely to be implemented if both parties agree it

Caution needs to be taken however as:

- The manager may not have the high level of skill that coaching feedback requires

- The review subject is unlikely to see their manager as impartial and may feel pressured by the process

- It can be challenging if there is conflict between the two of them

- The reporting relationship may make the review subject reluctant to discuss areas of weakness with their manager

THREE-WAY FEEDBACK REVIEWS

It can be useful to have a three-way feedback meeting between the review subject, their manager and an independent feedback coach. This is particularly appropriate where the review subject's manager needs to be involved but does not have sufficient experience to act as the feedback coach.

A three-way review can also be very useful if there is a poor relationship between the manager and the review subject and a degree of mediation is required.

THE FEEDBACK PROCESS

FEEDBACK REVIEW AGENDA

The feedback coach should:

- Choose a comfortable environment free from interruptions
- Explain the format of the interview and the intention of creating an action plan
- Discuss the review subject's expectations of how the feedback will help them (a positive attitude will result in greater willingness to take action afterwards)
- Present the report, explain what each section contains and check understanding. It helps if the initial training has contained a sample report
- Allow them time to read each section and ask questions
- Ask them to identify key points and themes emerging, rather than continuously making suggestions

THE FEEDBACK PROCESS

FEEDBACK REVIEW AGENDA

The feedback coach should:

- Act as an advocate for the feedback; don't allow the review subject to dismiss it just because they disagree
- Look for specific evidence of behaviours in the feedback
- Discuss the strengths identified at least as much as the development points
- Encourage the review subject to summarise regularly and make notes of action to be taken
- Explore the connection between the feedback and implications for business performance

THE FEEDBACK PROCESS

ANALYSING THE FEEDBACK

OVERALL LEVEL OF SCORES

Key things to look for when analysing the feedback report are:

- The overall level of scoring for competencies
- Differences in responses by different groups of respondents (peers, team members, etc)
- The relative scores given by different reporting groups
- Scores for the most important competency items for the review subject's job

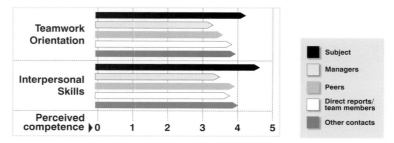

THE FEEDBACK PROCESS

ANALYSING THE FEEDBACK
OVERALL LEVEL OF SCORES

Questions to ask

- Are the overall scores high, low or medium against expectations?
- Is there a pattern in the overall responses?
- Why are there differences between the review subject's scores and those of others?
- Why should there be differences between different groups?
- Do the scores show obvious competency strengths or weaknesses?

THE FEEDBACK PROCESS

ANALYSING THE FEEDBACK
DIFFERENCES IN SCORES ON INDIVIDUAL ITEMS

	Self	Managers			Peers			Team members			Norm group score	Average
Mentors and coaches others	2	3	3	3	4	4	U	4	3	5	3.2	3.4

Questions to ask

● Why are there differences between the review subject's scores and those of others?

● Why should there be such difference of opinion from within the same group?

● Why should there be differences between different groups?

● Why are some people not able to comment on this item?

THE FEEDBACK PROCESS

ANALYSING THE FEEDBACK

REVIEW SUBJECT'S COMMENTS

In any 360 review, it is important to start from the frame of reference of the review subject. The comments they have offered about themselves when completing the questionnaire are thus the obvious place to start.

Questions to ask

- Why have they identified the points they have?

- Which competency areas have they concentrated on?

- Are there areas that they haven't commented on?

- Are there other points they could have identified?

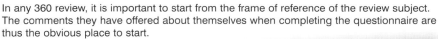

What do you consider are your key strengths?

I believe I have a high level of technical awareness in my job. I try hard to keep up to date with the latest developments in my field.

I usually manage to come up with solutions that are well received by my clients.

I keep good control of all the paperwork and systems associated with my projects.

I am financially aware and work hard at bringing in projects on time and to budget.

THE FEEDBACK PROCESS

ANALYSING THE FEEDBACK
OTHERS' WRITTEN COMMENTS

Questions to ask

- Do common themes recur?
- Do the comments support the scores given in the competency areas?
- Do the comments match those of the review subject?
- Are there any obvious differences between respondents' feedback and the review subject's self-image?

*Don't over-emphasise items that only occur once. Often these represent an isolated viewpoint. Be aware of them, but concentrate primarily on the repeated messages.

What are John's key development needs?

Being able to manage a team of engineers in the most effective way, this includes delegation of tasks.

His organisation and time-keeping skills.

The ability to manage time and prioritise needs attention.

Write shorter reports.*

Delegation/organisational skills (geared to his role as Project Manager).

Arrive to work on time, it sends the wrong message to others.

(Note that **time management** and **delegation** crop up repeatedly.)

ANALYSING THE FEEDBACK

DEALING WITH NEGATIVE COMMENTS

One of the best ways of avoiding destructive feedback is to get the review subject to nominate who will be their respondents and to be **personally** involved in inviting them to participate. When respondents see that they are being invited by a colleague, rather than an administrator, they are much more likely to offer constructive comments.

However, even when you have done this, provided training and briefing to respondents, and have worded your questions to draw out constructive feedback, there will be occasions when negative or destructive feedback is obtained. Sometimes this might be a badly worded comment, or it could be that someone is taking the opportunity to unload a long-held grudge. They could simply be having a bad day! Typically, such comments will be included in the section on the review subject's development needs.

THE FEEDBACK PROCESS

ANALYSING THE FEEDBACK

DEALING WITH NEGATIVE COMMENTS

- Remind the review subject that any negative comments in this section have come from the same people who provided the positive comments in the question on strengths

- Explore whether there is ambiguity in what is being said: could it be a constructive comment that is badly worded?

- Explore with the review subject why they think the respondent said what they did

In the case of particularly destructive comments, it might be appropriate for the scheme administrator to intervene before the final production of the feedback report. They then have the option to strike out the comments or refer them back to the respondent for review.

THE FEEDBACK PROCESS

KEY SKILLS FOR THE FEEDBACK COACH

- Being prepared
- Setting the scene and establishing expectations
- Building rapport
- Empathising – understanding **why** something is being said as well as **what** is being said
- Indicating respect
- Active listening
- Being aware of body language messages
- Acknowledging the review subject's views and priorities
- Checking assumptions
- Asking quality questions
- Providing a focus on the most important areas
- Taking time to fully explore issues
- Extrapolating and summarising

THE FEEDBACK PROCESS

THE JOURNEY TO ACTION

There are four stages to people taking action based on 360 review feedback:

Understanding what the feedback is saying

Accepting the feedback as other people's valid perceptions/opinions

Wanting to take action

Taking action

The coach has an important role to play in taking people through these four stages.

REACTIONS TO FEEDBACK

360 review is one of the most powerful experiences a person can have in the workplace and it can evoke strong emotions. The coach needs to respond appropriately. Above all else – listen.

Emotion/Reaction	Response
Dismissive	Get review subject to acknowledge the validity of others' views; act as an advocate for their views
Defensive, resistant	Explore underlying reasons for concern
Shifting the blame to others	Explore their personal role and responsibilities; what could **they** have done differently?
Angry	Stay calm; explore the reasons for the anger; get review subject to identify possible reasons for the feedback
Surprised	Investigate why there is a lack of awareness of the issues raised
Seeking to rationalise	Help test validity of any excuses made to explain the feedback
Emotional	Reassure the review subject that it's OK to be emotional; explore the reasons for the reaction
Elated	Don't allow the positive feedback to mask any development points
Motivated	Use this energy to fuel support for an action plan

THE FEEDBACK PROCESS

QUALITY COACHING QUESTIONS

- Why should people see you differently from how you see yourself?
- Why should there be differences in the different reporting groups' perceptions?
- What stops people from giving you this type of feedback more regularly?
- How can you capitalise on the strengths identified in the review?
- What will be the consequences of not changing performance in the areas that need development?
- What actions can you take to change people's perceptions of you?
- Who can you enlist to help you with your development plans?
- What other resources do you need to help you achieve your objectives?
- On a scale of 1 (not much interested) to 10 (top priority), how committed are you to making the agreed changes to your performance?

THE FEEDBACK PROCESS

TOP TIPS FOR FEEDBACK COACHES

- Always start with an exploration of the review subject's expectations
- Provide the coaching feedback promptly after collecting the responses. This will capitalise on the momentum built up and ensure the feedback is still relevant in fast-moving organisations
- Make sure enough time is allocated for the feedback. If the process is rushed or cut short, valuable discussion points may be lost. Two hours is a typical length of time for a good review but it may take longer
- Stress the developmental nature of the process, particularly if feedback is perceived as negative
- Help the review subject to make sense of poorly worded or ambiguous feedback comments
- In organisations with more open cultures, encourage the review subject to explore further the meaning of the feedback with his or her respondents. It may help if the coach facilitates this discussion

SUMMARISING FEEDBACK

A 360 degree feedback report is likely to contain a wealth of useful information. It is therefore useful for the coach to help the review subject to identify the **key** themes emerging. This is best achieved by getting the review subject to identify points in their own words. Areas that should be explored are:

- What are the key strengths identified?
- What are the key development areas suggested?
- What feedback can you set aside as not very important?
- What new questions does the feedback suggest?
- What areas of the feedback remain unclear?

Answers to these questions can form the basis of a personal development plan.

THE FEEDBACK PROCESS

PERSONAL DEVELOPMENT PLANS

Feedback is only meaningful if it results in **change**. When used to help an individual develop their skills there should **always** be a personal development plan (PDP). The priority activities in the personal development plan should be those that:

- Have the biggest personal impact on work-based performance
- Will receive the greatest level of commitment from the review subject

Find ways of increasing motivation	**High priority for the PDP**
Take no action	Nice to do but low priority

Business impact (vertical axis)

Personal motivation (horizontal axis)

PERSONAL DEVELOPMENT PLANS

The characteristics of good development objectives are:

- They are stated in simple language that can be understood by everyone

- They are about **outcomes** not actions – for example, *'attend a presentation skills course'* is not a development objective, it is a possible action on the journey towards the objective of: *'be able to deliver effective formal presentations in a variety of business settings'*

- They are stated in such a way that it can later be seen if they have been achieved or not

- They have a realistic timeframe for achievement

- They are limited in number – behavioural changes require considerable commitment from the review subject

Try to limit the number of development objectives to a maximum of four or five at most. One or two are fine if they are important enough.

THE FEEDBACK PROCESS

BUILDING ON THE POSITIVES

There is a tendency for the feedback review to focus on development needs. It's as important, and sometimes more important, to focus on the key strengths identified.

It is often much easier to build on strengths than address weaknesses and so the personal development plan should contain items on how the review subject can use and grow their existing talents in new ways.

SET 'DREAM IT©' OBJECTIVES

FEEDBACK PR

ING PERS

- **D**evelopmental – The actions should result in an improvement in performance for the individual

- **R**elevant – Focus on the key areas that will make a major difference

- **E**xciting – Objectives will not be met if the review subject is not motivated to achieve them. Choose only objectives where there is real commitment

- **A**chievable – Ensure actions are realistic in terms of what can be achieved given the available resources of time, money and commitment from others

- **M**easurable – Identify ways of measuring the difference (improved feedback, client satisfaction, business goals achieved, lower costs, etc)

- **I**ntegrated – Ensure objectives complement each other and are not mutually exclusive

- **T**ime framed – Set a clear target date for completion

© *Tony Peacock*

THE FEEDBACK PROCESS

SHARING PERSONAL DEVELOPMENT PLANS

If the manager is not acting as the feedback coach it is **essential** that the **personal development** plan is discussed with them to ensure:

- They understand the reason for the objectives in the plan
- They are in agreement with the priorities set
- Personal objectives fit in with wider business plans
- The plan feeds into any more general performance appraisal process
- They have an overview of all such plans within their team and how they fit together with their team priorities
- They allocate appropriate resources to help the review subject achieve the plan
- They offer support and guidance for achievement of objectives
- They help monitor progress

THE FEEDBACK PROCESS

CONFIDENTIAL DOESN'T MEAN SECRET!

The feedback report is given to the review subject in confidence, but that doesn't mean they have to keep its entire contents secret from others. Sharing key themes can be a good way to initiate a discussion with colleagues about how to develop.

Sharing results is about seeking further clarification and guidance, not trying to find out who said what. A useful approach is for the review subject to go back to their respondents, thank them for participating, and start to talk about ways to improve.

'My feedback suggested people would like me to communicate better. What could I do to help make this happen?'

'People suggested I could delegate more – can we discuss possible areas where I could do this?'

'Apparently I don't use my negotiating skills enough; when and where could I do this more?'

The feedback report itself should **not** be shared. Others will not have had the benefit of discussion with the coach and will have no way of understanding the learning that has been gained by the review subject. Sharing the report can also put unfair pressure on others to do likewise.

KEY ISSUES

LEGAL MATTERS

Your 360 feedback process should comply with your organisational policies and all appropriate legislative requirements. In particular:

- Does your questionnaire contain only questions that are relevant to the review subject's working life?

- Is there appropriate access available for people with visual or other impairments to participate in the review process?

- Does the storage of 360 review responses and reports comply with your organisation's data protection policy and data protection legislation?

- Are your feedback coaches suitably experienced/trained/qualified to facilitate the feedback?

- Do you have a mechanism to check that the feedback report does not contain anything that breaches the law on libel or discrimination on the basis of gender, race, culture, faith, age, sexual orientation?

WHEN NOT TO USE 360 FEEDBACK

360 feedback is a constructive process for personal development. Using it in another context will bring the process into disrepute and will usually have no benefit. Do not use it:

✗ Where there has been insufficient training/briefing on the purpose of the process

✗ To gather 'evidence' of poor performance

✗ As a substitute for managing the individual

✗ As part of a grievance or disciplinary process

✗ As part of a process involving salary considerations

✗ Where the review subject is not voluntarily taking part in the process

✗ Where there is a blame culture or a climate of fear that feedback will be used against people

✗ In highly dysfunctional teams or where there is conflict in the team

✗ Without an experienced feedback coach or facilitator to help the review subject process the feedback

✗ Where there is no commitment to follow up in terms of time and resources

LINK TO FINANCIAL REWARD

Some appraisal or performance review schemes are directly linked to financial reward through the awarding of pay increases or bonuses based on the result of the review.

360 review should **never** be used as a basis for financial reward; it is about **personal development**. The whole process will become distorted if the review subject sees it as being about achieving a 'successful' 360 review. If their future salary is involved it is unlikely that people will nominate any respondents other than those who will give them glowing comments!

USING 360 REVIEW WITH TEAMS

A 360 review can usefully be run to get feedback on the performance of a team. The process is exactly the same as for individuals, although different types of questions are used. The results can form the basis of a team development session with an appropriate development plan.

	strongly disagree	disagree	undecided	agree	strongly agree
The team is focused on their customers	◯	◯	◯	◯	◯
Individual skills and talents are fully utilised	◯	◯	◯	◯	◯
The team experiments with new ideas to improve services	◯	◯	◯	◯	◯
The team is proactive in getting customer feedback	◯	◯	◯	◯	◯
The team has clear business objectives	◯	◯	◯	◯	◯
The team helps members realise their potential	◯	◯	◯	◯	◯

EVALUATING THE PROCESS

REVIEW SUBJECT

The final stage, as with any developmental process, is evaluation to check that the procedure added value to the individual and the organisation. The first stage of this is to explore the review subject's perceptions of the process. A short post-review questionnaire can be used.

360 review evaluation: review subject

The questionnaire items were relevant to my work

strongly disagree ◯   disagree ◯   unsure ◯   agree ◯   strongly agree ◯

Overall the results increased my awareness of my strengths

strongly disagree ◯   disagree ◯   unsure ◯   agree ◯   strongly agree ◯

Overall the results increased my awareness of my development needs

strongly disagree ◯   disagree ◯   unsure ◯   agree ◯   strongly agree ◯

EVALUATING THE PROCESS
REVIEW SUBJECT

360 review evaluation: review subject

The feedback has motivated me to change certain behaviours in my work

strongly disagree ○   *disagree* ○   *unsure* ○   *agree* ○   *strongly agree* ○

The 360 review was an important development opportunity for me

strongly disagree ○   *disagree* ○   *unsure* ○   *agree* ○   *strongly agree* ○

In general the feedback I received was:

very unexpected ○   *somewhat unexpected* ○   somewhat expected ○   *expected* ○

What was the most important part of the feedback?

What would you change about the process?

EVALUATING THE PROCESS

RESPONDENTS

Feedback can also be obtained from respondents, particularly the subject's manager.

360 review evaluation: review subject's manager

The questionnaire items were relevant for my team member
strongly disagree ○ *disagree* ○ *unsure* ○ *agree* ○ *strongly agree* ○

The 360 review was an important development opportunity for my team member
strongly disagree ○ *disagree* ○ *unsure* ○ *agree* ○ *strongly agree* ○

I am confident that my team member will make appropriate behavioural changes as a result of the review
strongly disagree ○ *disagree* ○ *unsure* ○ *agree* ○ *strongly agree* ○

I have already seen appropriate behavioural changes in my team member
strongly disagree ○ *disagree* ○ *unsure* ○ *agree* ○ *strongly agree* ○

The feedback has motivated me to change certain behaviours in my own work
strongly disagree ○ *disagree* ○ *unsure* ○ *agree* ○ *strongly agree* ○

I have seen my team member's personal development plan   *Yes* ○ *No* ○

I have discussed my team member's personal development plan with them   *Yes* ○ *No* ○

EVALUATING THE PROCESS
REPEATING REVIEWS

Repeating a review after 12 months is a great way to measure the impact of the first review and resulting progress. Scores on competency ratings can be compared, and written comments can be explored to see if issues that were raised in the previous review have been commented on again, hopefully as areas that have improved!

INVESTING IN DEVELOPMENT

THE 80/20 RULE

There is little point in doing a 360 review if the organisation isn't committed to following up by providing the time and resources for participants to carry out their personal development plan.

360 review often addresses very fundamental issues that other development activities don't pick up on and you may be faced with changing very ingrained behaviours. If you are truly committed to helping your people to develop their skills you must be prepared to invest time, money and energy in helping them achieve their goals.

Out of all the resources allocated to the 360 review process, 80% should be spent on the follow up development activities compared with 20% required to run the process.

AND FINALLY!

360 degree feedback review is one of the most powerful development interventions that you can provide for your people. Setting up a scheme may seem daunting at first but the benefits are huge. Once your scheme is established you can use the system over and over again with many people in your organisation.

The wealth of constructive feedback that can be provided by a properly designed and implemented scheme can have a profound effect on motivating people and inspiring them to develop their skills, knowledge and attitude. Go for it!

About the Author

Tony Peacock, BA MA FCIPD

Tony is a highly experienced management and leadership trainer who has worked with many international organisations. He has sought to help many small and medium enterprises (SMEs), charities and other not for profit organisations with limited resources, to develop the skills of their people through low cost programmes.

In recent years Tony has specialised in introducing 360 degree personal development reviews into many organisations and has been involved in providing feedback coaching to hundreds of managers and leaders. He firmly believes that a well facilitated 360 degree review process can be a major development intervention and his PDR360Review suite of questionnaires is now used extensively in the UK.

In addition to developing and facilitating training programmes, Tony is a regular speaker at conferences and seminars; he has also written management and leadership articles for journals and magazines. He firmly believes that any development intervention should be inspirational and fun and his high energy training programmes have attracted warm praise.

Contact

Tony Peacock, Peacock Training Ltd
The Old Barn, Showell, Chippenham, Wiltshire, England SN15 2NU   Tel: 44 (0)1249 444661
tony@peacocktraining.co.uk   www.PDR360Review.co.uk

THE MANAGEMENT POCKETBOOK SERIES

Pocketbooks

360 Degree Feedback
Appraisals
Assertiveness
Balance Sheet
Business Planning
Business Writing
Call Centre Customer Care
Career Transition
Coaching
Communicator's
Competencies
Controlling Absenteeism
Creative Manager's
C.R.M.
Cross-cultural Business
Cultural Gaffes
Customer Service
Decision-making
Developing People
Discipline
Diversity
E-commerce
Emotional Intelligence
Employment Law
Empowerment

Energy and Well-being
Facilitator's
Flexible Workplace
Handling Complaints
Icebreakers
Impact & Presence
Improving Efficiency
Improving Profitability
Induction
Influencing
International Trade
Interviewer's
I.T. Trainer's
Key Account Manager's
Leadership
Learner's
Manager's
Managing Budgets
Managing Cashflow
Managing Change
Managing Difficult Participants
Managing Recruitment
Managing Upwards
Managing Your Appraisal
Marketing

Meetings
Mentoring
Motivation
Negotiator's
Networking
NLP
Openers & Closers
People Manager's
Performance Management
Personal Success
Positive Mental Attitude
Presentations
Problem Behaviour
Problem Solving
Project Management
Quality
Resolving Conflict
Sales Excellence
Salesperson's
Self-managed Development
Starting In Management
Strategy
Stress
Succeeding at Interviews
Talent Management

Teambuilding Activities
Teamworking
Telephone Skills
Telesales
Thinker's
Time Management
Trainer Standards
Trainer's
Training Evaluation
Training Needs Analysis
Virtual Teams
Vocal Skills

Pocketsquares

Great Training Robbery
Hook Your Audience

Pocketfiles

Trainer's Blue Pocketfile of
Ready-to-use Activities

Trainer's Green Pocketfile of
Ready-to-use Activities

Trainer's Red Pocketfile of
Ready-to-use Activities

21.5.07

ORDER FORM

Your details

Name _____

Position _____

Company _____

Address _____

_____

_____

Telephone _____

Fax _____

E-mail _____

VAT No. (EC companies) _____

Your Order Ref _____

Please send me:

	No. copies
The 360 Degree Feedback Pocketbook	
The _____ Pocketbook	
The _____ Pocketbook	
The _____ Pocketbook	
The _____ Pocketbook	

Order by Post

MANAGEMENT POCKETBOOKS LTD

LAUREL HOUSE, STATION APPROACH,
ALRESFORD, HAMPSHIRE SO24 9JH UK

Order by Phone, Fax or Internet

Telephone: +44 (0)1962 735573
Facsimile: +44 (0)1962 733637
E-mail: sales@pocketbook.co.uk
Web: www.pocketbook.co.uk

MANAGEMENT POCKETBOOKS